W9-CDW-564

(13)

(J)

Christmas in Mexico

by Cheryl L. Enderlein

Content Consultant:
Cyretta Chaput
Public Relations Officer
Mexican Cultural Institute

Hilltop Books

An Imprint of Franklin Watts
A Division of Grolier Publishing
New York   London   Hong Kong   Sydney
Danbury, Connecticut

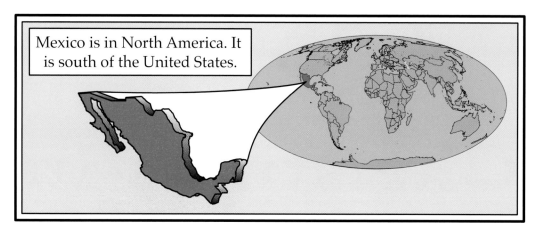

Mexico is in North America. It is south of the United States.

Hilltop Books
http://publishing.grolier.com
Copyright © 1998 by Capstone Press • All rights reserved
Published simultaneously in Canada• Printed in the United States of America

Library of Congress Cataloging-in-Publication Data
Enderlein, Cheryl L.
    Christmas in Mexico/by Cheryl L. Enderlein.
    p. cm.--(Christmas around the world)
    Includes bibliographical references and index.
    Summary: Describes the customs, songs, food, and activities associated with the
celebration of Christmas in Mexico.
    ISBN 1-56065-622-0
    1. Christmas--Mexico--Juvenile literature. 2. Mexico--Social life and customs--Juvenile
literature. [1. Christmas--Mexico. 2. Mexico--Social life and customs.] I. Title. II. Series.
GT4987.16.E56   1998
394.2663'0972--dc21
                                                    97-9400
                                                      CIP
                                                       AC

Photo credits
Vint Blackburn, 16
FPG/J. Pickerell, 8
Ernest Jones, cover
Ricardo Moura, 4, 12, 14, 20
Trip Photographic Library/C. Caffery, 6
Geoff Winningham, 10, 18

Table of Contents

Christmas in Mexico

Christmas is a holiday that is celebrated around the world. Celebrate means to do something enjoyable on a special occasion. People in different countries celebrate Christmas in different ways.

Mexico is a country in North America. It is south of the United States. People from Mexico are called Mexicans. They speak Spanish. Their Christmas greeting is Feliz Navidad (fay-LEEZ nah-vee-DAHD). It means Happy Christmas.

Christmas Day is always celebrated on December 25. But celebrations in Mexico start on December 16. This is the beginning of the nine days of posada (poh-SAH-dah). The celebrations end on February 2. This day is called Dia de la Candelaría (DEE-yah DEH LAH cahn-deh-LAH-ree-yah).

The weather in Mexico at Christmas time is mild. Mild means the days are warm, and nights are cool.

People in Mexico decorate for Christmas with lights.

The First Christmas

Many Christmas celebrations are part of the Christian religion. A religion is a set of beliefs people follow. Christians are people who follow the teachings of Jesus Christ. They celebrate Christmas as Jesus' birthday.

Jesus' mother was Mary. She was married to Joseph. Mary and Joseph traveled to the city of Bethlehem. They could not find any room at the inns. An inn is like a hotel. Mary and Joseph had to stay in a stable. A stable is where animals are kept.

Jesus was born in the stable. His first bed was a manger. A manger is a food box for animals. The manger was filled with straw.

Wise men brought gifts for Jesus. They followed a bright star. The star led them to Jesus.

Many Christmas celebrations remind people of the first Christmas. Most celebrations in Mexico are Christian.

People in Mexico set up figures to remember the Christmas story.

Symbols of Christmas

A special symbol of Christmas in Mexico is the poinsettia. A symbol is something that stands for another thing. The poinsettia is a plant with colored leaves. The leaves are red, pink, or white.

The poinsettia is named after Joel Poinsett. He was the first U.S. ambassador to Mexico. An ambassador is a person sent by a government to represent it in another country.

The poinsettia reminds many Mexicans of a special Christmas story. The story tells about a boy on Christmas Eve. He was going to church to visit baby Jesus. He wanted to bring a gift for Jesus. But the boy was poor. He did not have a gift.

The boy saw some green plants on the side of the road. He picked some and brought them to the church. Something special happened when he gave the plants to Jesus. The leaves on top of the plants changed color. They turned bright red.

Poinsettias are special Christmas symbols in Mexico.

Decorations

People in Mexico decorate their houses for Christmas. They shop for decorations at Christmas markets. People decorate with flowers, moss, and evergreens. Evergreens are plants that always stay green. People also decorate with many poinsettias.

Poinsettias are sometimes called the Flower of the Nativity. Nativity means the story of Jesus' birth. People also put out figures of Mary, Joseph, and the baby Jesus. This is called a nativity set or a manger scene. Many nativity sets also have figures of the wise men. Sometimes they have animals and other people from the Christmas story.

Paper lanterns are other Christmas decorations used in Mexico. A lantern is like a lamp. People also hang up Mexico's flag. The flag is red, white, and green. These colors are Christmas colors.

Mexicans shop for decorations at Christmas markets.

Christmas Celebrations

Mexicans have a posada on each of the nine nights before Christmas. Posada means inn in Spanish. A posada is like a game of hide and seek. The first posada is held December 16.

Children go from house to house. They carry small figures of Mary and Joseph. They pretend to look for a place to sleep. Many people send them away. The children try to find the one house that will let them in. There is a party when they find it.

The children put the figures of Mary and Joseph in the manger scene. Then, they try to break open a piñata (peen-YAH-tuh). A piñata is made of paper and paste. It is filled with candy and small gifts. The children hit the piñata with a stick. When it breaks, the candy and gifts fall out.

The last posada is on Christmas Eve. Children carry a figure of baby Jesus, too. They place him in the manger at the last house.

Children go from house to house on each night of posada.

Christmas Songs

Every country has special songs to sing at Christmas. In Mexico, children sing special songs during the posada.

The children sing as they walk from house to house. They sing at each house. The song asks the owner of the house for a room in the inn.

The owner answers them with a song, too. This song tells the children to go away. The owner says there is no room. The children keep trying different houses until they find the right one. There, the owner sings a song of welcome. The song says the children can come in.

There is another special posada song. Children sing this song on the last night. It is a lullaby for Jesus. A lullaby is a quiet song. It is sung to put babies to sleep. Children sing it to the figure of the baby Jesus. They ask him to sleep in his manger bed.

Children sing a song at each house, asking to come in.

Santa Claus

The first Santa Claus was a man named Saint Nicholas. A saint is a special person in the church. Saint Nicholas lived a long time ago. He secretly gave gifts to children and poor people.

A few children in Mexico believe in Santa Claus. These children usually live in big cities. They believe Santa Claus brings presents on Christmas Eve. The children open their presents that same night.

But many children in Mexico do not believe in Santa Claus. They believe in the Three Kings instead. The Three Kings are the wise men from the Christmas story. These children usually live in villages or in the country. The Three Kings bring them presents on January 6. They do not receive presents on Christmas Eve.

Most children believe the Three Kings bring them presents.

Christmas Presents

People all over the world give gifts at Christmas. Giving gifts reminds Christians of the wise men's gifts. The wise men brought special gifts to Jesus when he was born.

Most children in Mexico open their presents on January 6. This is the day Christians believe the wise men visited Jesus. This day in Mexico is called the Feast of Three Kings.

Children put their shoes out before they go to bed on January 5. They put their shoes on a window sill. The sill is the bottom part of the window. In the morning, the children's shoes are filled with presents. These presents are from the Three Kings.

Children put their shoes on the window sill to be filled with presents.

Holiday Foods

People in Mexico have special dinners on Christmas Day. They eat turkey, fruit, and vegetables. They also eat tortillas (tor-TEE-yahs). A tortilla is a type of bread. It is round and flat.

Mexicans also eat a special Christmas salad. It is called ensalada navideña (ehn-sah-LAH-dah nah-vee-DAY-nyah). The salad has fruit, beets, nuts, and sugarcane in it. Colored marshmallows are on top of the salad. Marshmallow is a soft, white candy.

Another Christmas food in Mexico is buñuelos (boo-NYWAY-lohs). Buñuelos are thin, round cakes. They are covered with cinnamon and sugar.

One Christmas food in Mexico is buñuelos.

Hands On: Make a Piñata

A piñata is a special part of the posada. You can make a piñata and play the piñata game.

What You Need

A balloon	String	Newspaper
A container	Wallpaper paste	Candy
A blindfold	Long stick	

What You Do

1. Blow up the balloon. Decide which part of the balloon will be the top of the piñata.
2. Cut two long pieces of string. Tie the strings around the balloon. Wrap each piece around the balloon like you are wrapping a present. The ends should be at the top you have chosen. Leave the ends long. You can use them to hang up the finished piñata.
3. Cut or tear the newspaper into long strips.
4. Cover the table with more newspaper. The next part is messy.
5. Put the wallpaper paste in a container. Dip one newspaper strip into the paste. Put it on the balloon. Keep doing this. Overlap the strips. Make three or four layers. Leave a hole at the top. Do not cover up this part. You need the hole to fill the piñata.
6. Let the newspaper dry.
7. Pop the balloon. You can decorate the piñata if you like.
8. Fill the piñata with candy. Hang it up using the string.
9. Take turns being blindfolded. Try to hit the piñata until it breaks.

Words to Know

Christian (KRISS-chuhn)—a person who follows the teachings of Jesus Christ

evergreen (EV-ur-green)—a plant that stays green all the time

inn (IN)—a place to sleep overnight like a hotel

manger (MAYN-jur)—a food box for animals

poinsettia (poin-SET-uh)—a plant with colored leaves on top

posada (poh-SAH-dah)—Spanish word for inn; also a special Mexican Christmas celebration

stable (STAY-buhl)—a building for animals like a barn

Read More

Cuyler, Margery. *The All-Around Christmas Book*. New York: Holt, Rinehart and Winston, 1982.

Fowler, Virginie. *Christmas Crafts and Customs*. Englewood Cliffs, N.J.: Prentice-Hall, 1984.

Lankford, Mary D. *Christmas Around the World*. New York: Morrow Junior Books, 1995.

World Book. *Christmas in Mexico*. Chicago: World Book, Inc., 1995.

Useful Addresses and Internet Sites

The Embassy of Mexico
1911 Pennsylvania Avenue NW
Washington, DC 20006

Mexican Cultural Institute
2829 16th Street NW
Washington, DC 20009

Christmas.com
http://www.christmas.com

Christmas 'round the World
http://www.auburn.edu/%7Evestmon/christmas.html

A Worldwide Christmas Calendar
http://www.algonet.se/~bernadot/christmas/info.html

Index

Boston Public Library

FIELDS CORNER
BRANCH LIBRARY